Developing Literacy
SENTENCE LEVEL

SENTENCE-LEVEL ACTIVITIES FOR THE LITERACY HOUR

year

6

Christine Moorcroft

Series consultant:

Ray Barker

A & C BLACK

Reprinted 1999
Published 1999 by
A&C Black (Publishers) Limited
35 Bedford Row, London WC1R 4JH

ISBN O-7136-5174-1

The author and publisher would like to thank Ray Barker
and the following teachers for their advice in producing this
series of books: Tracy Adam; Hardip Channa; Lydia Hunt;
Madeleine Madden; Helen Mason; Judith Metcalfe; Heather Morrealy;
Yvonne Newman; Hilary Walden; Fleur Whatley; Annette Wilson.

The author wishes to thank Magnus Magnusson for permission to use the
paraphrased extract from *Egil's Saga* and for supplying the Icelandic words (page 9).

A CIP catalogue record for this book is
available from the British Library.

Printed in Great Britain by
St Edmundsbury Press Ltd, Bury St Edmunds, Suffolk.

Contents

Introduction

Developing Literacy: Sentence Level supports the teaching of reading and writing by providing a series of activities to develop children's understanding that grammar is about the way in which we combine words in sentences to enable the reader to understand what we have written: that writing must make sense to the reader as well as to the writer. To understand grammar, children need to know about the different types of words which make up sentences.

The children learn to examine the effect of their choice of words and to question whether it communicates what they intend. They find out how their choice affects the audience. They also investigate the effect of changing the order of words in a sentence and how to make a text suitable for a particular audience and purpose. They develop their ability to use punctuation to make sentences show variation which would otherwise only be possible in speech.

The activities are designed to be carried out in the time allocated to independent work during the Literacy Hour. They support the objectives of the National Literacy Strategy *Framework for Teaching* at sentence level and incorporate strategies which encourage independent learning – for example, ways in which children can check their own work or that of a partner. Particular emphasis is given to investigating language at **Year 6**.

Year 6 helps children to develop:

• an understanding of elements of grammar introduced in **Years R,1,2,3,4** and **5** and –

    other forms of English;
    how to construct complex sentences;
    how to write in the impersonal voice;
    how to organise long sentences;

• an understanding of sentence-construction and punctuation introduced in **Years R,1,2,3,4** and **5** and –

    connective words and phrases;
    how to use commas, colons, semi-colons, dashes and brackets;
    the effects of sentence-structure and punctuation on meaning;
    different types of clause;
    how to use conditional verbs;
    how to make notes and summarise;
    editing;
    how to use the impersonal voice and the passive voice in writing.

The following logos are used to remind the children to use references such as dictionaries and thesauruses:

Year 6 encourages the children to investigate language: the effect of re-arranging the clauses in a sentence and changing its punctuation; different forms of English; the use of active and passive verbs in different types of text and the type of language used in different contexts.

Extension

Most of the activity sheets end with a challenge (**Now try this!**) which reinforces and extends the children's learning and provides an opportunity for assessment. These more challenging activities might be appropriate for only a few children; it is not expected that the whole class should complete them. On some pages there is space for the children to complete the extension activities, but others will require a notebook or separate sheet of paper.

Organisation

For many of the activities it will be useful to have available scissors, glue, word-banks, thesauruses, a variety of dictionaries and fiction and non-fiction texts of a variety of genres: for example, journals, newspapers and letters. To help teachers to select appropriate learning experiences for their pupils, the activities are grouped into sections within each book. The pages do not need to be presented in the order in which they appear in the book, unless otherwise stated.

Teachers' notes

Brief notes are provided at the bottom of most pages. They give ideas and suggestions for making the most of the activity sheet. They sometimes make suggestions for the whole class introduction, the plenary session or, possibly, for follow-up work using an adapted version of the activity sheet.

Structure of the Literacy Hour

The following chart shows an example of the way in which an activity from this book can be used to achieve the required organisation of the Literacy Hour.

Shortening sentences (page 54)

Whole class introduction	**15 min**
Read a selection of extracts from shared texts which contain long sentences, some of which might be unpublished sources such as letters, or examples made up by the teacher. Include long descriptive sentences from authors such as Charles Dickens, George Eliot and J R R Tolkien. Ask the children to identify the extracts which should be left unaltered, and to say why. Discuss the information which is conveyed to the reader and the mental image and the feeling or atmosphere created by long passages. The children should be able to identify texts which are intended to convey a simple message and in which detail is unnecessary and can even obscure the message.	

Whole class activity	**15 min**
Set up a 'sentence-shortening department' in the classroom: a group of able children is seated at the front of the class, while the others take turns to read out long sentences from cards (previously prepared by the teacher) which need to be shortened. Members of the 'sentence-shortening department' have to give (verbally) the shortened sentences. Examples of sentences to be shortened: 'I would be very grateful if you could tell me where the nearest telephone is because my friend has broken his leg'; 'Would you please chase that young woman who has stolen my handbag?'; 'I have left my watch at home and so I would be most grateful if you would look at yours and tell me what time it is'.	

Group work	**20 min**	**Independent work**	**20 min**
The children match a set of shortened sentences to their original, long versions and decide which should be shortened, which should be left as they are and why, and in which contexts it is appropriate to use particular sentences. (Include sentences from novels.)		The others work independently from the activity **Shortening sentences** (page 54, **Developing Literacy Sentence Level: Year 6**).	

Whole class plenary session	**10 min**
The children share and compare their shortened sentences and begin to analyse the kind of changes which they have made: for example, deleting descriptions and using one or two words instead of several.	

Using the activity sheets

Grammatical awareness

This section provides activities which develop the children's grammatical awareness by drawing attention to styles of writing, the conventions of standard English, how to adapt texts to suit audiences, contexts and purposes, how to construct sentences which convey the writer's intended meaning and how to use punctuation to avoid ambiguity and promote clarity. It also consolidates the children's understanding of classes of words and encourages them to explore and enjoy language.

Word classes (page 9) consolidates the children's understanding of nouns, adjectives, verbs and prepositions by asking them to investigate, from the surrounding text, the part of speech of a word which they are unlikely to be able to read or understand. The extract from *Egil's Saga* uses Icelandic words for this purpose, while providing an example of a genre which might be new to the children. The Icelandic words are translated as follows: put, shield, head, sword, pulled, slammed, head, wide, bushy, nose, full beard, chin, jaws, massive, neck, thick, shoulders, heavy, drooped down, cheek, lifted, hair, eyes, black, eyebrows, drink, served, twitched, down, sword, scabbard, took, fine, large ring, arm, slipped, point, up, reached, towards, through, towards, put, ring, arm, eyebrows, level, sword, helmet, ale-horn, drank.

Preposition proverbs (page 10) consolidates the children's understanding of prepositions and helps them to understand that a preposition shows a relationship between two ideas.

Investigate: Word-order (page 11) helps the children to express the same idea in different ways and thus to be in a position to choose which is the better or best for a particular context or purpose. In **Investigate: Compound sentences** (page 12) the children learn to construct compound sentences by combining simple sentences. These then become clauses of compound sentences (sentences with two or more main clauses). In **Investigate: Complex sentences** (page 13) the children add subsidiary clauses to simple sentences. A subsidiary clause acts as the direct object of the verb in the main clause: for example, I have a feeling that I have been here before.

Using adverbs (page 14) revises adverbs in a way which also helps the children to recognise and use standard English. **Investigate: Forms of English** (page 15) revises agreement of pronouns with verbs in standard English. **Investigate: Standard English** (page 16) includes examples of the use of non-standard English which is influenced by dialect. It helps the children to recognise the differences between this dialect-influenced English, which can be understood even by people who are unfamiliar with the dialects in question, and standard English. Non-standard English is not necessarily 'wrong' – it is often used in poetry and drama – but frequently, as in this example, it features non-agreement between verbs and nouns or pronouns, double negatives, non-standard use of words, and dialect and slang words. The children are required to identify and classify these deviations from standard English.

Adapting a text (page 17) develops the children's ability to match the structure, language and grammar of a text to its audience, purpose and context.

Active sentences (page 18) develops the children's understanding of active verbs and of the terms 'subject' and 'object'. They should notice that in active sentences and clauses the subject precedes the verb and the object (if there is one) follows it. **Passive sentences** (page 19) develops the children's understanding of how to use verbs in the passive voice. They should notice that, as in active sentences, the subject precedes the verb, but it has the action done *to* it. They could investigate the use of the passive voice in texts such as reports, where the action is more important than who does it. (See also page 63.) **Active to passive** (page 20) requires the children to consider the changes which must be made when an active sentence is made passive. **Investigate: Active and passive** (page 21) develops the children's understanding of the construction of active and passive sentences. They should compare the effect on the reader of a sentence in the active and then in the passive voice, and decide which is the more appropriate. They should consider this in their own writing. For the extension activity, provide texts such as leaflets and certain types of instructions which are written in the passive.

Official language (page 22) encourages the children to think about the meaning of a text and then to simplify it. For homework the children could collect and bring to school examples of official language, for 'translation' in class. For the extension activity, provide official texts such as competition forms, photographs of signs and notices and leaflets about special offers or promotions. **Investigate: Official words and phrases** (page 23) is about the vocabulary of official language. The children should have the opportunity to investigate the vocabulary used on a variety of official forms; they could make a word-bank of 'official' vocabulary. **Personal and impersonal** (page 24) develops the children's appreciation of the differences between personal and impersonal language. The children might notice that many 'official' documents, such as information leaflets from banks and building societies, are written in personal language to make them seem more friendly as well as to make them easier to understand. (See also page 62.)

Imperative verbs (page 25) revises the imperative form of verbs and encourages the children to explore their use in texts such as notices and instructions. (See also page 28.) In **Investigate: Narrative texts** (page 26) the children learn to recognise who is the narrator of a narrative from clues such as the pronouns used and the person in which the text is written. They develop awareness of the effects which can be created by the author's choice of narrator. **Writing a recount** (page 27) requires the children to write about a series of events in chronological order. In the extension activity they should notice differences between each type of recount. In **Writing instructions** (page 28) the children should read the entire set of instructions before they begin to re-write them, and then make rough notes about the order in which the sentences are to be presented. They might need to devise a system of checking that they have not omitted anything, perhaps by asking a friend to follow their instructions. In **Investigate: Reports** (page 29) the children explore the language, grammar and other features of factual reports. They should notice that, unlike recounts, reports are usually written in the present tense; but like recounts they are factual and so are written in language which is clear and unambiguous. Unlike recounts, they are not presented in chronological order (because they do not describe events). However, when the children write their own complete reports, they need to present them in a logical order, with an introduction and a structure which the reader can easily follow. They might also find it useful to include headings. **Explanations** (page 30) develops the children's skills in organising notes to write an explanation. Before beginning the activity, they should explore the features of different kinds of explanatory texts, such as dictionaries and information books. During a group reading session the children could make notes about features such as the tense used, whether the language is formal or informal, personal or impersonal, in which person the texts are written and the vocabulary used. In **Investigate: Persuasion** (page 31) the children should notice that persuasive texts are usually written in the present tense and make use of logical connectives. In **Investigate: Promotional texts** (page 32) they learn to recognise the ways in which a persuasive text is written to appeal to a certain audience. They should notice that the first leaflet, with its formal language and serious tone, is written to attract adult visitors (or school parties) who want to learn and do not require to be entertained, whereas the second, with its informal language and its use of questions and humorous challenges, is written to attract young adults and families with children who want an exciting day out. **Discussion** (page 33) provides an opportunity to revise direct and reported speech, and for the children to consider more interesting alternatives to 'said'. They also need to consider how to introduce and summarise the discussion.

Investigate: Different forms of English (page 34) is about words in everyday use in English, both within and outside the United Kingdom. The *Collins English Dictionary (Millennium Edition)* is a useful reference source for the main activity. During the extension activity children who have lived in, or whose families are from, other English-speaking countries, could help the others by supplying examples. **Investigate: Technical language** (page 35) is about the technical language (or jargon) used by people who share the same activities or employment. The children should find that in most technical language it is mainly the nouns and verbs which are specialised (although sometimes specialised adjectives are used to describe conditions); they might realise that this is because technical language needs words for equipment and activities. For the extension activity, provide books about the subjects listed. **Investigate: English from the past** (page 36) uses the language of Tudor England to develop the children's understanding of the ways in which English has changed (and is still changing). The written 16th century language looks difficult, but once it is read aloud its meaning becomes much clearer. The meanings of some words can be worked out from the context of the surrounding text. If the children still have difficulties, the following glossary will help: array (dress), cappe (cap), fayre (well), keame (comb), kye (cow), nayles (nails), ordain (send), rayment (raiment – clothing), se (see), syc up (strain), yf (if), ynke (ink). In **Investigate: The language of proverbs** (page 37) the children examine the way in which proverbs are written in relation to their purpose (to pass on wisdom). They should notice that proverbs are usually statements or instructions in the present tense. The instructions are written in the second person, as are some of the statements. All the proverbs in the examples have active verbs which can be positive or negative. **Investigate: The language of jokes** (page 38) develops the children's understanding of what makes a joke funny. The first three items in the key depend on the use of language, while the last two depend on logic. During the extension activity the children might find some jokes which do not fit into any of the categories in the key; if so, discussion of their ideas should help them to make up a new category. In **Investigate: The language of headlines** (page 39) the children explore the sources of humour in headlines while developing their knowledge of homophones, homonyms, puns, idioms and sayings.

Sentence-construction and punctuation

Connective words and phrases (page 40) revises the use of connectives to link ideas which might be expressed as phrases, clauses or sentences. A connective word or phrase can be placed at the beginning of a sentence. This activity also develops the children's understanding of the different types of connectives and their purposes. **Investigate: Connectives in various texts** (page 41) encourages the children to examine the types of connectives which are useful in different kinds of texts; for example, logical connectives are useful in arguments and time connectives in recounts. **Investigate: Connectives in a recount** (page 42) develops the children's understanding of the functions of connectives in recounts. The children could discuss the replacement of some connectives by dates and times in order to make a recount more precise. **Investigate: Connectives in an argument** (page 43) provides a structure for preparing an argument. It is closely connected to text-level work (see also page 33), but its sentence-level focus is the function of connective words and phrases in an argument.

Using colons (page 44) revises the use of the colon to introduce a list. Discuss with the children the different ways in which lists can be introduced. **Using semi-colons** (page 45) revises the use of semi-colons which can replace connective words and phrases to join two clauses. The children might notice in their reading that sometimes a semi-colon precedes a connective word or phrase. **Lists** (page 46) revises the use of colons to introduce, and commas to separate, items in a list. It introduces the use of semi-colons to separate long items in a list. During a group reading activity the children could compare the ways in which different writers punctuate lists. Useful texts for this purpose include extracts from novels (not necessarily written for children) which contain long sentences, instructions, recipes, information leaflets and legal documents.

Investigate: Commas for separating (page 47) revises the use of commas to separate parts of a sentence in a way which communicates its meaning to the reader. The children could try putting a comma in various places in the sentences and then reading them aloud to a partner, who has to say where the comma is. **Commas and meaning** (page 48) develops the children's understanding of the use of commas in conveying the intended meaning of a sentence. **Dashes for separating** (page 49) helps the children to enlarge their repertoire of punctuation marks. In some sentences a colon or even a comma can be used instead of a dash or, where two dashes are used, the words between the dashes can be enclosed within brackets. In **Brackets** (page 50) the children learn to use brackets for surrounding an additional piece of information which is added to a sentence and without which the sentence still makes sense grammatically and logically. A pair of commas or dashes can often be used for the same purpose.

Clauses (page 51) revises clauses and develops the children's ability to use connective words and phrases to combine clauses in sentences. The children could explore the effects of changing both their choice of connective words and phrases and the order in which they place the clauses. **Constructing complex sentences** (page 52) develops the children's understanding of complex sentences and helps them to use them in their writing.

Short forms (page 53) provides some standard abbreviations which can help to speed up note-making. It introduces the idea of non-standard abbreviations which are meaningful to the writer and which can become standard within a group of users. **Shortening sentences** (page 54) develops the children's ability to extract the main points from a sentence so that they can communicate information briefly and effectively or make notes for their own use in writing a report or other text. Useful books for the extension activity include those by Charles Dickens, George Eliot and J.R.R. Tolkien. The children should be aware of what is lost when they shorten sentences from fiction, while appreciating that their summaries are useful ways of describing the main events of the story. **Avoiding repetition** (page 55) develops the children's skills in writing concisely. It could be introduced by listening to recordings of news on the television or radio during which the children could notice the ways in which repetition is avoided: for example, by using collective nouns. The children could also spot any repetition (a common one is 'am' and 'in the morning' or 'pm' and 'in the evening'). **Summaries** (page 56) helps the children to analyse the process of summarising by considering a series of questions. Similar questions can be used in the analysis of most texts and the resulting notes can then be used to inform the summary itself.

Auxiliary verbs (page 57) develops the children's understanding of the use of auxiliary verbs in making continuous tenses. **Conditional clauses** (page 58) introduces conditionals by focusing on the conditional clause itself, which usually begins with 'if' or, occasionally, 'unless'. The children can complete all of these sentences with an 'if' or 'unless' clause. **Conditional songs and rhymes** (page 59) develops the children's understanding of conditionals by introducing a focus on the verbs, including (in the extension activity) their tenses. **Conditional verbs** (page 60) develops the children's ability to use conditional verbs. It is a challenging activity in which they must pay close attention to the tenses of the verbs. **Just suppose** (page 61) encourages the children to use conditionals to talk about probability and to express hypotheses.

Formal writing (page 62) consolidates the children's understanding of the imperative forms of verbs and the impersonal voice. Provide formal texts for the group reading session such as safety instructions from hotels, ships and aircraft, rules from various organisations and 'small print' from forms. In **Using passive verbs** (page 63) the children revise the use of the passive and develop an appreciation of the purposes for which it is used. **Better sentences** (page 64) draws upon and consolidates a number of aspects of writing: punctuation, clauses and compound and complex sentences. The activity helps the children to understand the purpose of punctuation, and develops their ability to construct sentences which convey the intended meaning to the reader.

Glossary of terms used

abbreviation A shortened form. Sometimes an apostrophe is used to denote letters which are omitted; for example, *can't*.
active When a verb is active the subject of the sentence performs the action; for example, <u>Dan</u> built a wall.
adjective A word which describes (qualifies) a noun; for example, *big, sweet, soft*.
adverb A word which qualifies a verb; for example, *quickly, sadly*.
agreement The way in which linked words agree with one another in terms of person, gender, singular or plural, and tense.
ambiguity This occurs when text has more than one possible meaning.
auxiliary verb One of a small group of verbs which combines with a main verb to make a tense, or to make the main verb passive; for example, *We <u>were</u> walking to school/I <u>have</u> eaten the cake/She <u>was</u> bitten by a dog.*
clause A group of words which is a distinct part of a sentence and can act as a sentence. A clause includes a verb.
colon (:) A punctuation mark mainly used to introduce a list or an identification (information which is needed to answer a question implied in the first part of the sentence); for example, *We saw three kinds of tree: an oak, an elm and a rowan.*
comma (,) A punctuation mark which is used to separate or surround parts of a sentence and items in a list.
complex sentence A sentence which contains a main clause and at least one subordinate clause.
compound sentence A sentence which contains more than one main clause.
conjunction A word used to link sentences or clauses or to connect words within the same phrase; for example, *and, but*.
connective A word (or phrase) which makes a connection between one phrase, clause, sentence or paragraph and another. A connective can be a conjunction or an adverb, a prepositional expression or a pronoun.
contraction A shortened form (using an apostrophe to denote omitted letters) of a word or words; for example, *don't*.
dash (–) A punctuation mark which can be used to indicate an afterthought or hesitation or, in pairs, to replace brackets.
derivation The origin of a word or saying.
dialect A form of a language which usually belongs to a region and has non-standard forms of grammar and vocabulary.
genre A specific type of writing or other medium of communication; for example, legend, newspaper story or poem.
homonym A word which has the same spelling as another but a different meaning.
homophone A word which sounds the same as another.
imperative The form of a verb which is used for giving orders, commands, requests or instructions.
interrogative The form of a verb used in questions.
intransitive verb A verb which has no object.
jargon Language used by a particular group of people which might not be understood by others.
main clause A clause which makes sense on its own, logically as well as grammatically.
object The recipient of an action; for example, *Mum read the <u>newspaper</u>.*
parentheses () Brackets.
parenthesis A word or phrase inserted into a sentence to explain or elaborate. It can be placed between commas, dashes or brackets.
passive The form of a verb which is used when the subject has the action done to him, her or it; for example, *She <u>was bitten</u> by a dog.* Sometimes the agent who or which carries out the activity is not given; for example, *Heads <u>shall</u> roll.*
person A text may be written in the first person, the second person or the third person.
personal pronoun (see **pronoun**).
phrase A group of words which act as a unit; for example, *the old man went to sleep <u>in his chair</u>.*
possessive pronoun (see **pronoun**).
possessive The form of a noun which shows ownership: *Jane's, the girl's, the children's, the boys'.*
preposition A word which describes a relationship between one noun or pronoun (or noun or pronoun phrase) and another; for example, *before, on, under*.
pronoun A word used instead of a noun, for example: (personal pronouns) *I, you, he, she, it, we, they*; (dependent possessive pronouns) *my, your, her, his, its, our, their*; (independent possessive pronouns) *mine, yours, his, hers, its, ours , theirs*.
semi-colon (;) A punctuation mark used to separate clauses of equal importance in a sentence.
statement A sentence which gives information: for example, *He likes reading.*
subject The subject of a verb is the person or thing which does it: for example, *<u>Mum</u> read the newspaper.*
subordinate clause A clause which does not make sense, logically, on its own – it depends for its meaning on a main clause; for example, *I shall write to you as soon as <u>I know when the wedding is to be.</u>*
tense The tense of a verb shows when it happens; for example, (present) *she <u>writes</u>/she <u>is writing</u>*, (past) *she <u>wrote</u>/she <u>has written</u>*, (future) *she <u>will write.</u>*

The passage has been translated from an Icelandic saga. Some Icelandic words have been left in.

- Work out what class of word each Icelandic word is.
- Underline each class of word in a different colour.

Key

nouns
adjectives
verbs
prepositions

Egil sat down and **skaut** his **skjöldur** at his feet. He had his helmet on his **höfuð.** He laid

Complete the key to show which colours you will use.

his **sverð** across his knees and now and again he **dró** it part of the way out of the scabbard, then **skelldi** it back in again. He sat bolt upright, but his **höfuð** was bowed low. Egil had a **breitt** forehead, **þykkvar** eyebrows and a broad **nef**. He had a very **stört skegg**. His **haka** and **kjálkar** were **mikil**, his **háls** was **digr** and his **herðar** were **þungar**.

As Egil sat there, one eyebrow **hleypði niðr** to his **kinn** and the other **hljóp** to the roots of his **hár**. His **augu** were **svört** and his **augabrún** joined in the middle. He refused to **drekka** although it was **borit** to him, but **hleypði** his eyebrows up and **niður** in turn.

Then King Athelstan drew his own **sverð** from its **slíður** and **tók** a **góðan**, **stóran hring** from his **hönd**, and **dró** it over the **blóðrefill** of his sword; he stood **upp** and **rétti** across with it **til** Egil. Egil put his own sword-point **í bug** the ring and lifted it **að** him.

Egil **dró** the **hring** on his **hönd** and his **augabrún** became **í lag** again. He put down his **sverð** and his **hjálm** and picked up the **dyrshorn** and **drakk** from it.

PARAPHRASED FROM A TRANSLATION BY MAGNUS MAGNUSSON OF *Egil's Saga*, CHAPTER 55.

Now try this!

- **Re-write the passage, replacing the Icelandic words with English words of the same class.**

Teachers' note The children should be able to work out, from the surrounding text, to which class of word each of the Icelandic words belongs. The surrounding text should also give them clues for English words which would make sense in their place.

Developing Literacy
Sentence Level Year 6
© A & C Black 1999

9

Preposition proverbs

- **Complete each proverb with a preposition.**

Use a dictionary of proverbs.

1. Don't put the cart _____ the horse.

2. It's no use crying _____ spilt milk.

3. Make hay _____ the sun shines.

4. There is honour _____ thieves.

5. Don't count your chickens _____ they are hatched.

6. A stitch _____ time saves nine.

7. There is no smoke _____ a fire.

8. Don't hide your light _____ a bushel.

9. It's easy to be wise _____ the event.

10. You can not burn the candle _____ both ends.

11. _____ the cat's away, the mice will play.

- **In each proverb what items or ideas are linked by the preposition? Record them on a chart.**

Now try this!

Proverb	Item/idea 1	Item/idea 2
①	the cart	the horse

Teachers' note In the extension activity the children could also describe the type of relationship which the preposition shows between the two items or ideas. Ask them whether the prepositions show 'how', 'when', 'where' or 'why'.

Developing Literacy
Sentence Level Year 6
© A & C Black 1999

Word-order

• **Write each sentence in a different way: change the word-order but keep the same meaning.**

> You can add, remove or change some of the words.

Example:

A famous writer lived in the High Street.	In the High Street there lived a famous writer.

1. Pizza, salad, sausages and sardines are my favourite foods.

<u>My favourite...</u> _____

_____

2. The most famous painting in the world is the 'Mona Lisa'.

3. We were late because we did not set out soon enough.

4. The cheapest form of exercise is walking.

5. If the Rovers win the double I'll eat my hat!

6. In 1805 Horatio Nelson was killed at the Battle of Trafalgar.

Now try this!

• **Re-write a short piece of your own work, changing the order of the words in some sentences.**

• **With a partner, decide which word-order sounds best.**

Teachers' note In some of their other written work the children could try writing the sentences in different ways and then selecting the one which they prefer. Ask them to explain their choices or to say if two ways of writing a sentence have equal merit.

Developing Literacy
Sentence Level Year 6
© A & C Black 1999

Compound sentences

- **Untangle the text.**
- **Build compound sentences using the simple sentences as clauses.**

<u>Jones took a free kick.</u> The telephone rang. We arrived at the station at two o'clock. <u>The ball landed at the feet of Smith.</u> There was a train at the platform. It was Rani. It was going to Manchester. Lisa ran as fast as she could. He dodged four defenders. She invited us to her party. It was due to leave in one minute. She did not win the race. She had done her best. He scored a brilliant goal. She was happy.

Useful connectives

and	but
who	which
so	then
because	

You might need to change some personal pronouns to 'who' or 'which'.

1. (4 clauses) <u>Jones took a free kick and the ball landed at the feet of Smith...</u>

2. (3 clauses) _____

_____

3. (4 clauses) _____

_____

_____

4. (4 clauses) _____

_____

_____

Now try this!

- **Write four simple sentences about any topic.**
- **Re-write the sentences as clauses of a compound sentence. Use some of the connectives on the note pad.**

Underline the verbs.

Teachers' note The children could identify compound sentences in a shared text: ask them to look for sentences which have more than one clause. Can all the clauses be written as separate sentences? If so, they are main clauses.

Developing Literacy
Sentence Level Year 6
© A & C Black 1999

Complex sentences

I know that.

What do you know?

I know that snails are gastropods.

Simple sentence   **Complex sentence**

- **Make the simple sentences into complex sentences by adding a clause.**

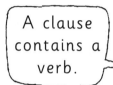

A clause contains a verb.

1. I have a feeling _____

2. I heard that _____

3. They were quick to notice that _____
_____

4. He understood that _____

5. The gardener told me that _____
_____

6. The fortune-teller predicted that _____
_____

7. The shepherd counted _____

8. An old man sitting on the bench watched _____
_____

9. Jenny and Omar sang _____

10. The manager told me that _____

Now try this!

- **Circle the main verb in each sentence. Underline the clause which is the object of that verb.**

Ask the question 'what?'

Teachers' note The children should first complete page 12. Ask them to compare their compound and complex sentences and to describe the differences between them. They should notice that complex sentences contain at least one clause which would not make sense logically as a sentence.

Developing Literacy
Sentence Level Year 6
© A & C Black 1999

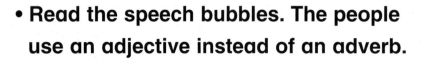
- **Read the speech bubbles. The people use an adjective instead of an adverb.**
- **Underline the verbs in each speech.**
- **Circle the adjective which should be an adverb.**
- **Write the adverb underneath.**

> An adverb says something about a verb.

The lads <u>played</u> (good).

She sings so sweet.

I can type very quick.

The lads played well. _____ _____

Make sure you write neat.

Don't walk so slow.

He swam as strong as he could.

_____ _____ _____

I crashed the car because I drove careless.

He talks so quiet that I can hardly hear him.

He was sobbing pitiful because he was lost.

_____ _____ _____

- **Underline the verbs in a piece of your own writing.**
- **Write an adverb to describe each verb.**

Teachers' note It might be necessary to revise adjectives before the children begin this activity, which can be linked with word-level work on making adverbs from adjectives.

Developing Literacy
Sentence Level Year 6
© A & C Black 1999

14

Forms of English

- **Read the words of the twelve-year-old street crossing-sweeper.**
- **Complete the chart to compare the speech with modern standard English.**

Mother's been dead these two year, sir, and father's a working cutler, sir; and I lives with him, but he don't get much to do, and so I'm obligated to help him, doing what I can sir... I've had to mind my little brother and sister, so that I haven't been to school; but when I goes a-crossing-sweeping I takes them along with me, and they sits on the steps close by, sir. If it's wet I has to stop at home and take care of them... Sister's three-and-a-half year old and brother's five year, so he's just beginning to help me, sir.

FROM *London labour and the London Poor* BY HENRY MAYHEW (1861)

Victorian crossing-sweeper	Modern standard English
these two year	for two years

Now try this!

- **Describe how the Victorian crossing-sweeper's speech is different from modern standard English.**

Teachers' note If necessary, point out the plural nouns and agreement between verbs and their subjects. The children could try writing in the style and language of the Victorian crossing-sweeper.

Developing Literacy
Sentence Level Year 6
© A & C Black 1999

Standard English

- **Underline the parts of the passage which are not in standard English.**

"Hi!" Clare called to Deepak, "I thought I seen you over there, but I <u>weren't</u> sure. Did you go to the match on Saturday?"

"No, I never went," said Deepak, "I didn't have no money. Me mates went. I asked me dad if he'd borrow me the money, but he were skint."

"Our Jane were there," said Clare. "She said that penalty shouldn't never have been given. Owen couldn't of handled the ball because his hands was in the air and the ball weren't nowhere near them."

"Me dad said Owen done the right thing to shut up, though," said Deepak. "He don't never argue with refs, even if they don't know nothing."

- **In the columns on the chart, write the words which you underlined to show how they differ from standard English.**

Pronoun and verb do not agree	Noun and verb do not agree	Double negative	Dialect or slang word
I weren't			

- **Look at another text which contains non-standard English. List the examples of non-standard English.**
- **Explain why the writer did not use standard English.**

Teachers' note The children might notice other examples of non-standard English in the passage, such as the wrong tense of the verb being used ('I seen'), non-agreement of pronoun and noun ('me mates') and dialect phrases ('couldn't of').

Developing Literacy Sentence Level Year 6 © A & C Black 1999

16

Adapting a text

- **Use the information in the notebook to write a glossary about river animals and fish.**

Remember to arrange your glossary in alphabetical order.

By the river we saw some mammals. One was a brown rat. It had a long tail with no fur on it, a pointed snout and quite large, rounded ears. There was a water vole too, which was brown, like the rat, and had a similarly shaped body, but its ears were smaller, its snout was blunt and it had a furry tail. There was a water shrew which had greyish-black fur and a long, pointed snout. As well as the mammals, we saw some fish: a school of dace with long, streamlined, silvery bodies were swimming near the surface of the water. They each had one small dorsal fin and two small fins on the underside of their bodies. A trout lurked at the bottom of the stream; trout have dark spots on their light creamy-brown bodies. One of the insects which we saw was a stonefly, which was light brown in colour and had laid its eggs under some stones, and some damselflies, which breed among the waterside plants.

Glossary

dace: freshwater fish with a long, streamlined, silvery body.

_____

_____

_____

_____

_____

_____

_____

_____

- **Make a glossary using information from your own science note book.**

Teachers' note Having looked at some glossaries in information books, the children should discuss the distinctive features of glossaries and the ways in which they are arranged in order to make reference quick and easy.

Developing Literacy
Sentence Level Year 6
© A & C Black 1999

Active sentences

- The [subject] of an <u>active sentence</u> (or clause) does the action. The [object] has the action done to it.
- Complete the sentences on the chart.

Subject	Verb	Object	Connective	Subject	Verb	Object
Sean's dad	bought	a car	but	he	did not like	it.
The angler	caught		and then		smiled.	
	drew		but		likes	
	likes		but		eat	
	eat		because		was raining.	
	wore		but		does not have	
	has		and		saw	
	opened					

- On a photocopied text, underline all the verbs. Circle the subject of each verb in one colour. Circle the object of each verb in another colour.

Teachers' note The children should understand the terms 'subject' and 'object' before they begin this activity. They could identify the subjects (and objects where appropriate) in a shared text.

Developing Literacy
Sentence Level Year 6
© A & C Black 1999

Passive sentences

In a <u>passive sentence</u> (or clause) the subject has the
action done to it.

Subject	Verb
The cake	had been eaten.

A passive
sentence need not
have an object.

• **Write some passive sentences.**

Subject	Verb		Object
The bread	was buttered.		
The bread	was buttered	by	Paul.
The grass			
The grass			
A window			
A window			
The door			
The door			
People			
People			
Two paintings			
Two paintings			
An old coin			
An old coin			

Now
try
this!

• **With a partner, look for passive verbs in different**
  kinds of texts.

• **Record them on a chart.**

Text	Subject	Passive verb	Object
Instructions	fire escapes	can be found	_____

Teachers' note The children should first complete page 18. Discuss the example sentence, in which
the reader is not told who had eaten the cake, and ask the children to look for other examples of
passive sentences which allow the object of the verb to be hidden.

Developing Literacy
Sentence Level Year 6
© A & C Black 1999

Active to passive

- **Re-write the information leaflet using passive verbs.**

Seaview Hotel

bathrobe - We have hung a bathrobe in the bathroom. You should leave it there. You can buy a bathrobe from reception.

hairdryer - We have provided a hairdryer for you to use during your stay.

housekeeping - You can obtain extra bedding or towels from the housekeeper.

laundry - The laundry can wash your personal items. Place them in the laundry bag and write your name and room number on it.

porter - The porters can provide assistance with your luggage.

restaurant - You can book a table in the restaurant by dialling 023.

room service - You can order meals and snacks by dialling 024.

A bathrobe has been hung in the bathroom. It should be...

Now try this!

- **Write five sentences, with active verbs, giving information about things you can do at your school.**
- **Re-write the information using passive verbs.**

Teachers' note The children should first complete pages 18 and 19. Read and discuss the use of passive verbs in shared texts such as hotel information leaflets and instructions to rail, air and sea travellers.

Developing Literacy
Sentence Level Year 6
© A & C Black 1999

Active and passive

- **Decide whether each sentence is active or passive.** ☐A or ☐P
- **Circle the verb.**
- **Underline the subject in blue and the object in red.**

> Remember – a sentence need not have an object.

☐A or ☐P	
	The telephone rang.
	The school bell was rung.
	I watched television.
	A new tax was introduced by the government.
	Mum whistled a tune.
	Send for details today.
	Drivers were confused by the new roundabout.
	Milk is tested for tuberculosis.
	Scientists are researching new fertilisers.
	His idea was considered.
	The letter had been delivered to the wrong address.
	Dogs are banned from this beach.
	Who has been eating my porridge?

- **What do you notice about the word-order of**
- active sentences? _____
- passive sentences? _____

Now try this!

- **Re-write a text which has passive verbs, making the verbs active.**
- **Make a note of any problems which you meet.**

Teachers' note The children should first complete pages 18–20. After the extension activity, discuss some of the problems encountered: for example, the lack of an object in some passive sentences, such as 'The school bell was rung' (who rang it?).

Developing Literacy
Sentence Level Year 6
© A & C Black 1999

Official language

- **Re-write the official language in everyday language.**

Use a dictionary.

Calls to mobile phones are not eligible for this offer.	You cannot use this offer when you call a mobile phone.

A free gift* with every purchase.
* Subject to availability

VEHICLES PROHIBITED

The company's decision is final and no correspondence will be entered into.

Winners will be notified by post.

Customers are requested to refrain from consuming food and beverages not purchased here.

Now try this !

- **Look for other examples of formal language.**
- **Copy them and explain what they mean.**

Text	Formal language	Meaning
Notice in a station	We apologise for any inconvenience caused by the building work.	We are sorry if the building work has made things difficult for you.

Teachers' note The children should first read, as shared texts, examples of official language in leaflets and brochures, and on pictures of signs. They could also compare informal and formal texts, noting the vocabulary used and the simplicity or complexity of sentences.

Developing Literacy
Sentence Level Year 6
© A & C Black 1999

Official words and phrases

This vehicle licence form has some words missing.

- **Write the missing official words in the gaps.**

Use a dictionary.

Official words

advance
declaration
effect
exempt
imprisonment
issued
maximum
overleaf
recommend
requires
valid
vehicle

A licence comes into force on the day it is _____ except when it is taken out in _____, in which case it takes _____ from the first day of the following month.

If the form _____ you to produce a test certificate it must be _____ on the day the licence comes into force. Certain vehicles are _____ from testing.

We _____ that you do not post cash unless you use registered post.

If your _____ is not used or kept on public roads you must make a _____. Make the declaration by putting a cross in the box on the form _____.

The _____ penalty for making a false declaration is £5,000 or two years' _____.

Now try this!

- **Learn the spellings and meanings of the official words.**
  - **Look** **Say** **Cover** **Write** **Check**
- **List ten other words from official documents.**
- **Write their meanings.**

LSCWCh

Teachers' note As shared texts, read examples of official documents such as instructions for completing forms (for example, census returns, electoral roll forms and television licence applications). Ask the children to point out any words they come across which are not used in everyday language. Do they know what they mean? They can check them in dictionaries.

Developing Literacy
Sentence Level Year 6
© A & C Black 1999

Personal and impersonal

- **Write the instructions in the impersonal voice.**

Think about making verbs passive, replacing 'you' with a plural noun and changing 'your' to 'their'.

① You should take off your shoes when you enter a mosque.

② You can buy a ticket here.

⑤ You must not smoke on the train.

③ You must not drive your car in the bus lane.

④ You must not go past this point unless you work here.

⑧ You may cash cheques here.

⑥ You must not bring dogs (except guide dogs) into the shop.

⑦ If you are a student you can have a discount.

1. <u>Visitors should remove their...</u> _____

_____

2. _____

3. _____

4. _____

5. _____

6. _____

_____

7. _____

_____

8. _____

Now try this!

- **Copy other examples of impersonal language.**
- **Re-write them in the personal voice.**

Look in official texts for your examples.

Teachers' note After completing the main activity the children could describe the types of changes which they made, such as replacing 'you' with a noun and 'your' with 'their' and, in some cases, making active verbs passive.

Developing Literacy
Sentence Level Year 6
© A & C Black 1999

• **Write the instructions using imperative verbs.**

You might need to change, add or remove words.

> People need to tick the YES box to order the Book of the Month. They put a cross in the NO box to reject it.

> To order other books they write the reference numbers of the books in the boxes.

> To order more than one copy of a book, they repeat the reference number the appropriate number of times.

> They write the price of the book in the space provided and add on the amount shown for postage. They write the total.

> They should write their membership number on the reverse of their cheque.

> They must return the form within ten days.

> They should keep a note of the titles ordered.

How to order books

To order the 'Book of the Month' tick the YES box; to reject it, put a cross in the NO box.

Now try this!

• **Collect five instruction leaflets or order forms and highlight the imperative verbs.**

• **Make a note of any other forms of verbs which you notice.**

Teachers' note The children might also notice the use of conditional verbs in official language: for example, 'If you wish to order two copies of a book you should ...'

Developing Literacy
Sentence Level Year 6
© A & C Black 1999

Narrative texts

The narrator of a story can be the author, or a character in the story.

- **Who is the narrator in these extracts?**

Mohandas Gandhi was born on 2nd October 1869 in Porbandar, a small state in north-west India.

"It's a very old tree," I said. "Yes," said Katy. "It's a yew. They live for ages. Did you know that, Sian?" "No," I replied.

There we waited, my brother and I, with hundreds of other children. All of us had labels pinned to our coats. Surely they didn't think we would forget our names?

_____   _____   _____

- **List some of the clues which tell you who the narrator is.**

_____

_____

_____

- **If the narrator is a character in the story, how does the author tell the reader that character's name?** _____

_____

_____

- **Investigate narrative texts.**
- **Record your findings on a chart like this.**

Text	Genre	Narrator	Clues
The Swallow and the Raven (Aesop)	fable	author	Written in third person and characters named.
Boy: Tales of Childhood (Roald Dahl)	autobiography	author	Written in first person. Main character ('I') not named except by other people.
Skellig (David Almond)	fantasy	Michael, a character in the story	Written in first person. Other characters use his name.

Teachers' note The children could discuss the effect of the choice of narrator and consider the effect of changing the narrator. They could change the narrator in the examples provided and notice the effect this has on other words in the sentences.

Developing Literacy
Sentence Level Year 6
© A & C Black 1999

Writing a recount

- **Write a recount of this incident for one of the drivers' insurance claim forms.**

I was driving along Low Road towards
High Street.
_____
_____
_____
_____
_____
_____
_____
_____

Think about:
- setting
  the scene
- tense
- chronological order
- pronouns
- accuracy of
  your description
- connectives
- summary

_____
_____
_____
_____
_____
_____
_____
_____
_____

Now try this!

- **With a partner, investigate recounts in journals, newspapers, diaries and letters.**
- **Highlight in different colours:** | verbs | | pronouns |

| connectives which show chronological order |

Teachers' note The children could compare the ways in which writers of recounts set the scene, convey chronological order and summarise. They could read their own recount to a partner who could help them to edit it.

Developing Literacy
Sentence Level Year 6
© A & C Black 1999

Writing instructions

- **Read the instructions for making patchwork.**
- **Re-write them in a way which is easier to follow.**

Patchwork

You should sew the fabric squares together in strips. It is best to begin by placing two fabric squares on top of one another with their fronts facing. Sew in backstitch in a straight line near the edge of the fabric. When you sew two strips together you need to put them with their right sides facing and stitch along one long edge of the fabric with backstitch. It is a good idea to cut out several squares of fabric before you start sewing. You need to cut a square of card 8cm x 8cm to use as a pattern for cutting squares of fabric. This needs to be pinned on to the fabric so that you can draw round it. The best fabric to use is cotton. It helps if you pin the squares together before you sew them.

You need

Stitches you will use

Teachers' note Read some instructions as a guided reading activity, asking the children about the features which help the reader: for example, lists of equipment and skills which will be used; imperative verbs and instructions written in step-by-step order.

Developing Literacy
Sentence Level Year 6
© A & C Black 1999

Reports

A <u>report</u> describes the way things are.

- **Read the extracts from reports and complete the chart.**

① Liverpool has several art galleries. The Tate, at Albert Dock, has a collection of modern art. The Walker has painting and sculpture from many periods, including 12th century Italian, 17th century Dutch and 19th century English art.

② The children's behaviour is very good. They are polite to one another, to teachers and to visitors. They co-operate in group tasks and share equipment.

③ The building is 80 years old and in a fairly good state of repair. It has been re-wired. The roof is in need of repairs; it has ten to twenty tiles missing and up to a quarter of the others are damaged.

④ Most of the inhabitants of the island are employed in fishing, agriculture or tourism, but there is a growing number of craftspeople: jewellers, potters, knitwear designers and perfumiers.

⑤ The Islamic calendar is calculated from the Hijrah (flight) of the Prophet from Makkah to Madina. The Hebrew calendar dates from when the world was thought to have begun.

	Tense	Subject	Person	Information given
1.				The number of art galleries in Liverpool and the type of art they house.
2.				
3.				
4.				
5.				

Now try this!

- **Compare these reports with the recounts which you investigated. List the similarities and differences.**

Teachers' note The children should first have completed page 27. They could compare other reports and allocate points out of five to them for clarity of language. They should notice whether the language used in them is personal or impersonal and formal or informal.

Developing Literacy
Sentence Level Year 6
© A & C Black 1999

Explanations

Explanations answer questions.

- **Read Adam's questions and his dad's answers in note form.**
- **Decide on the best order for the points made in each explanation.**
- **Write the explanations in full.**

(1.) Why do some things float, but not others?

(2.) What is hayfever?

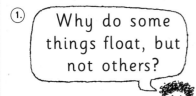

(1.) • Dense • Heavy for size • If less dense than water – will float; denser – will sink.

(3.) Why is the sky blue?

1. _____
_____
_____
_____
_____

(2.) • Eyes red+sore
• Mucus blocks breathing passages.
• Caused by allergy to pollen or other pollutants.

2. _____
_____
_____
_____

(3.) Mixture of all colours of rainbow = white. Sunlight made of all colours. Only blue light reflected downwards from gases in sky. Air made of gases.

3. _____
_____
_____
_____

Now try this!

- **Research an answer to this question and write an explanation for a partner to read.**

How are hailstones made?

Teachers' note Discuss the type of language which is suitable for explanations (clear and in the present tense) and the order in which the sentences should be presented, including an introductory sentence and, possibly, a summary sentence.

Developing Literacy
Sentence Level Year 6
© A & C Black 1999

Persuasion

- **Underline the opening statement of this leaflet.**
- **Number the points of the argument which the writer uses.**

  How many points are there? ☐

Our lifestyles can influence our health. People are different in ways they can't change – height, build, family medical history, disability and inherited diseases. However, there are things which people can change: for example, exercise, food, time spent in the sun and whether or not they smoke or drink alcohol. Many health problems do not affect people until late in life, but this does not mean that the diet and lifestyle which people have before that does not matter. By then a lot of damage might have been done. On the other hand, it is never too late to change; further damage can be prevented. Moreover, some damage can be undone: for example, if a lifetime of eating too much fat has led to unhealthy arteries, changing to a low fat diet can begin to undo some of the damage.

There is much conflicting advice on television and radio and in the press, but the real experts are in agreement about some things. There is some evidence, for example, that eating a diet high in fruit and vegetables and taking regular, moderate exercise are beneficial. So, although there are no hard and fast rules about health, there are basic guidelines.

- **Complete the chart.**

Verbs and tenses (pr = present, pa = past, f = future)	can (pr),
Connective words and phrases	however,

- **Write the conclusion of the argument.**

- **Read other persuasive texts and record your findings on charts like the one above.**

Remember to make a note of the title of each text.

Teachers' note The children could write a persuasive text connected with their work in another subject; for example, to persuade other children to take care of school property or to do things which contribute to care of the wider environment, or a letter to the local council to ask for footpaths to be created or improved.

Developing Literacy
Sentence Level Year 6
© A & C Black 1999

Promotional texts

- **Use the chart to compare these promotional leaflets.**

Discover Birmingham's Heritage

Soho House was the elegant home of the industrial pioneer, Matthew Boulton, from 1766 to 1809. Here he used to meet some of the most important scientists, engineers and thinkers of his time.

Soho House has been carefully restored to its 18th century appearance and contains some of Boulton's own furniture. Displays tell the story of this fascinating man and the interests he shared with his famous visitors. There is also the chance to see some of the products of Boulton's factory, where ormolu clocks and vases and the beautiful silver and Sheffield plate tableware were made and where he developed the steam engine with James Watt.

The Drayton Manor Experience!

Drayton Manor family theme park is no end of fun! On for a real day out? Then get down to Drayton Manor. There are big rides, fun rides and kiddie rides. Try the Shockwave. Will you dare do it? The Shockwave is definitely not for the faint-hearted. It's the only stand-up roller-coaster in Europe. White-knuckle? You'd better believe it!

Try the Haunting. You're not easily frightened, are you? So the idea of following in the footsteps of a special investigation team which has mysteriously disappeared wouldn't make your blood run cold? Prepare to chill out in the Haunting.

Audience	Soho House	Drayton Manor
Words which give clues about the audience.		
Is the language formal or informal? Give examples.		
Personal or impersonal language? Give examples.		

Now try this !

- **List some words and phrases which you could use in writing a promotional leaflet for a place you know.**

- **What conclusions can you draw about promotional language?**

Remember to write a heading for the leaflet.

Teachers' note As a group reading activity, the children could compare promotional leaflets from other places to visit and classify them according to whom they would attract and why. They should consider the language, grammar and vocabulary used, as well as any pictures.

Developing Literacy
Sentence Level Year 6
© A & C Black 1999

Discussion

A journalist interviewed local people to find their views about a new car factory.

- **Read the people's replies.**
- **Write a discussion about the factory.**

Useful words and phrases

welcomed	complained
were concerned	argued
opposed	expressed
looked forward to	

It will bring money into the area – a good thing.

I can't wait for it to open. I might get a job.

It's going to spoil a quiet country village. It will bring noise and traffic.

It will ruin the view from the village across to the hills.

I'm worried about the danger to children with all the extra traffic.

Maybe if there's a factory people will live here – instead of just having holiday homes here.

Yes – it will be nice to see people here on weekdays.

Me too.

Now try this!

- **Read other discussions and list the words which are used to introduce people's views.**

Use local newspapers.

Teachers' note Encourage the children to use the words on the notepad to avoid repetitive use of 'said'. This activity could be linked with other subjects in which the children can represent people's views as a discussion.

Developing Literacy
Sentence Level Year 6
© A & C Black 1999

Different forms of English

In other English-speaking countries, different words are used in everyday language.

- Match the American and Australian words to their English meanings.

Use a dictionary.

USA:
airplane
candies   ice box
faucet   sidewalk
French fries
hood (of a car)
trunk (of a car)

Great Britain:
tap
refrigerator
bag
bonnet
sweets
food   van
hello
sheep
boot
hire purchase
wellington boots
holiday home
pavement
aeroplane
chips

Australia:
goodday
gumboots   swag
jumbuck   tucker
layby   ute
weekender

Different words are used for the same thing even in different parts of the Great Britain.

- Write the standard English word (or phrase) for these:

bap, cob _____   felts, inkies _____

brass, readies _____   gormless, thick _____

butty, sarny _____   rooked, skint _____

caffle, dither, swither _____

daps, pumps, sandshoes _____

Now try this!

- **Investigate different forms of English words from places such as India, Jamaica, African countries and New Zealand.**

Teachers' note The children could compile Anglo-American and Anglo-Australian glossaries, using their knowledge of these forms of English gained from television programmes and films. They could also compile glossaries of slang words (remind them that slang words should not be used in their writing).

**Developing Literacy
Sentence Level Year 6
© A & C Black 1999**

Technical language

• **Match the language to the subject.**

Subjects
law
fitness instruction
gardening
medicine
chess

Tissue affected by sarcoid appears under the microscope to contain tubercles (or granulomas) but tubercle bacilli are not found.

_____

Let's take it from the top. One, two, three. Scoop to the right - and again. To the left. Then fishtail. Heel - toe, heel - toe.

_____

I give all my property not otherwise disposed of by this will or any Codicil hereto unto my Trustees upon trust to sell the same (with power to postpone sale).

_____

Propagate rhododendrons by layering...
Continue to prune shrubs...
Root the cuttings to be potted in the spring.

_____

I had to get the rook out.

You shouldn't have castled.

You could have sacrificed your king's pawn.

_____

• **Write the technical words on the chart.**

Subject	Verbs	Nouns
law		
fitness instruction		
gardening		
medicine		
chess		

Now try this!

• **Investigate the language of other subjects and record your findings on a chart.**

Look at books about the subjects.

Teachers' note The children could find the meanings of the technical words. They could re-write one of the technical texts in a way which does not use jargon – and thus realise why jargon has to be used in some instances (so that one or two words can be used instead of several).

**Developing Literacy
Sentence Level Year 6
© A & C Black 1999**

English from the past

- **Read these extracts from texts written in Tudor times.**
- **Highlight the words which are not in common use nowadays.**
- **Work out what they mean and list them in the glossary.**

Do not highlight words which are still in use but are spelled differently. Read the texts aloud – you will be surprised how much you understand.

Thy hands se thou washe, and thy head keame,
And of thy rayment se torne be no seame.
Thy cappe fayre brusht thy hed cover then
Tayking it of in speaking to any man…

A napkyn se that thou hast in redines,
Thy nose to clense from al fylthines.
Thy nayles, yf nede be se that thou payre,
Thine eares kepe clene, thy teath washe thou fayre.

This done, thy setchell and thy bokes take
And to schole haste se thou make.
But ere thou goest with thyselfe forethynke
That thou takest with thee pen, paper and ynke.

FROM *The Schole of Vertue* BY A F SEAGER (1557)

First in a morning when thou art waked, lift up thine hand and bless thee… then first sweep thy house, dress up thy dishboard and set all things in good order: milk thy kye, syc up thy milk, take up thy children and array them and provide for thy husband's breakfast, dinner and supper…ordain corn and malt to the mill, to bake and brew withal when need is…and se that thou hast thy measure again or else the miller dealeth not truly with thee. Thou must make butter and cheese…serve thy swine both morning and evening…

FROM *The Book of Husbandry* (FOR FARMERS' WIVES) BY AN UNKNOWN AUTHOR (1523)

Glossary

_____   _____

_____   _____

_____   _____

_____   _____

_____   _____

_____   _____

Now try this!

- **Re-write one of the texts in modern English.**

Teachers' note The children could also investigate the English of other periods of history which they are studying. Provide copies of the original texts and typeset transcriptions, and have available glossaries or modern versions of the texts.

**Developing Literacy
Sentence Level Year 6
© A & C Black 1999**

The language of proverbs

• **Read the proverbs. Use the chart to describe the language used in them.**

A sentence can be a statement, an instruction, a question or an exclamation.

1. Actions speak louder than words.

2. If the cap fits, wear it.

3. You can not get blood from a stone.

4. It's no use crying over spilt milk.

5. Many hands make light work.

6. Make haste slowly.

7. Never look a gift horse in the mouth.

8. You can take a horse to the water, but you can not make it drink.

9. Make hay while the sun shines.

10. Strike while the iron is hot.

	Type of Sentence	Positive or negative verbs	Active or passive verbs	Tense	Person
1.	statement	positive	active	present	third (plural)
2.					
3.					
4.					
5.					
6.					
7.					
8.					
9.					
10.					

Now try this!

• **Write the meanings of the proverbs.**

• **Find out about their origins.**

Teachers' note Before this activity it might be necessary to revise tense, person, different types of sentences and how to recognise them, as well as positive and negative statements and active and passive verbs.

Developing Literacy
Sentence Level Year 6
© A & C Black 1999

The language of jokes

- **With a partner, read the jokes aloud.**
- **In the box next to each joke, write a code from the key to show what makes the joke funny.**

Key

hn	homonym
hp	homophone
in	invented words
lo	logical, but unexpected, answers
mi	misunderstanding

A woman wanted to book a flight from London to Lahore. She phoned a travel agent and asked how long the flight would take.
"Just a minute," said the person who answered the phone.
"Thank you," said the caller, and hung up.

Knock, knock

Who's there?

Major!

Major who?

– Major answer the door, didn't I?

What's a forum?
– Two-um plus two-um!

Why do cows wear bells?
– In case their horns don't work!

What do pigs put on cuts?
– Oinkment!

What happens to a stone if you throw it into the Red Sea?
– It gets wet!

What's the Loch Ness Monster's favourite food?
– Fish and ships!

Why did the singer stand on a ladder?
– To reach the high notes!

In which battle was Nelson killed?
– His last one.

- **With a partner, write six other jokes you know.**
- **Use the key to show what makes them funny.**

Teachers' note For the extension activity provide books of jokes and encourage the children to look for jokes whose humour does not fit into the five categories outlined in the activity. The humour of each joke belongs to one main category, although there is some overlap. The answers are therefore open to discussion.

Developing Literacy
Sentence Level Year 6
© A & C Black 1999

The language of headlines

There is often humour in newspaper headlines.

- **Explain the play on words in these.**

Use a dictionary.

CHIP SHOP OWNER BATTERS MAN

_____
_____
_____

_____

_____

_____

MAGISTRATES ACT TO KEEP THEATRE OPEN

'PANDA'MONIUM
Our zoos are in a mess

_____

_____

WOMEN'S WRITES
Launch of book of poems and short stories by local women

PAIN STOPS PLAY
Cricketer bitten by adder

_____

_____

SOUND THE A-LLAMA
Farmer's pet frightens locals

MED TO MEASURE
Put together your own package holiday

_____

_____

Now try this!

- **Investigate other headlines. What types of news stories have humorous headlines? What makes them funny?**

Headline	Source of humour			
	Homonym	Homophone	Invented word	Well known phrase or saying
CHIP SHOP OWNER BATTERS MAN	Batter			

Teachers' note In the extension activity the children could discuss the appropriateness of humour in headlines, noticing that it is used mainly in connection with scandals or light-hearted matters; it is sometimes used to express an opinion about the actions of someone in the public eye, but never about sad events.

Developing Literacy
Sentence Level Year 6
© A & C Black 1999

Connective words and phrases

Connective words and phrases link ideas.

She put up her umbrella <u>so that</u> she would not get wet.

In this sentence the connective shows a purpose.

- **Complete the sentences with the type of connective shown in the headings. Use a different connective each time.**

Additional information

We can book your hotel, supply your travellers' cheques _____
_____

You might win a free holiday _____

Place

There was a harvest-mouse _____
A kestrel hovered _____
Squawking gulls flew _____ the tractor which chugged _____

Time

The man parked his car _____
He would leave it at the parking meter _____
_____ he would drive to Swansea.

Purpose, reason or logic

Working in noisy places can harm people's hearing _____
_____

Employers provide protective clothing _____
_____

_____ some employees do not use this protection.

Now try this!

- **Re-write one sentence from each set, using a different connective to change the meaning.**

Teachers' note After this activity, the children could read different kinds of texts and highlight the different types of connectives in different colours.

Developing Literacy
Sentence Level Year 6
© A & C Black 1999

Connectives in various texts

- **Underline the connective words and phrases in each text.**
- **Complete the chart.**

1

The kitchen has a range of quality base <u>and</u> wall units <u>together with</u> several built-in appliances. There is also a utility room and a separate boiler-house. On the first floor there are four bedrooms and a bathroom. The main bedroom has an en-suite bathroom with a jacuzzi.

2

When combined with other discounts the saving could be as much as 30%. What's more, Call+Save is FREE to join. So if your quarterly bill is between £25 and £70 you could benefit.

3

It's all very well knowing what you're supposed to eat, but putting this knowledge into planning meals is another matter. However, there are some guidelines which will help. First, you do not need to make detailed calculations.

4

No interest will be charged if the total balance is paid by the due date. You may wish, however, to pay part of the balance, in which case interest will be charged on the remainder.

5

The cat padded across the shady lawn until it reached a patch of sunlight. There it stretched luxuriously and then curled up to sleep. Before long its whiskers began to twitch and it batted something with its paw. Next it stood up and yawned and after a while it noticed that the patch of sunlight had shifted.

Text	Type of text	Types of connectives			
		Additional information	Place	Time	Purpose, reason or logic
1.	Report	and, together with			
2.	Promotional				
3.	Argument				
4.	Explanation				
5.	Recount				

• Investigate the types of connectives used in other texts and record them on a chart or in a database.

Teachers' note The children could also investigate the connectives used in different genres of fiction and poetry.

Developing Literacy
Sentence Level Year 6
© A & C Black 1999

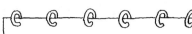

Connectives in a recount

- **With a partner, read the recount.**
- **Re-write it using connective words and phrases.**

A steam packet named *Forfarshire* left Hull at 6pm on 5 September 1838. The starboard boiler was leaking badly. The leak put out two of the furnaces. The vessel reached Berwick Bay. The sea became stormy. The leaking boiler became worse. The crew poured water into it. It poured out again. The engines could not be driven. The vessel drifted. It struck Great Harcar Rock. The crew called to the passengers. Few could hear them. Nine people scrambled from the wreck on to the rock. They had carried three others with them. These three had died. Grace Darling of the Longstone Lighthouse spotted the survivors. She and her father, William, rowed out to the rock. Her mother, Thomasin, prepared hot food and drinks. Grace's younger brother, William, was rowing to the wreck with the crew of the Sunderland lifeboat.

Useful connectives

after a while
after some time
afterwards
meanwhile
before long
eventually
immediately
in the meantime
finally   soon
later   then
already   and
next   but
so

Now try this !

- **Highlight the connectives in two different types of recount: for example, a newspaper story and a chapter of a novel.**
- **Swap over some of the connectives and compare the new versions with the originals.**

Teachers' note During a guided writing activity, the children could write their own recounts of an event they have witnessed, or an event in history, in simple, factual sentences, and then re-write it using connectives which help to show the sequence and timing of events.

**Developing Literacy
Sentence Level Year 6
© A & C Black 1999**

Connectives in an argument

- **Think of a plan to improve your school playground.**
- **On the notepads, write what four different playground users think of your plan.**
- **Complete the list of logical connectives which you could use in writing an argument about the improvement to the playground.**

Viewpoint 1

Name

Opinion

Reason

Viewpoint 2

Name

Opinion

Reason

Viewpoint 3

Name

Opinion

Reason

Viewpoint 4

Name

Opinion

Reason

Logical connectives

on the other hand
however

Use a thesaurus.

- **Number the viewpoints to show the order in which you will present them in your argument.**
- **Write your argument. Include an introduction and a summary.**

Now try this!

Teachers' note This activity should be linked to work outside the Literacy Hour. Before using the activity sheet, the children should make a survey of the opinions of playground-users. The activity can be linked with text-level work on writing an argument.

**Developing Literacy
Sentence Level Year 6
© A & C Black 1999**

Using colons

- **Some lists are introduced by a colon, others are not.**

The train stops at Runcorn, Crewe, Stafford and Wolverhampton stations.

These are the stations at which the train stops: Runcorn, Crewe, Stafford and Wolverhampton.

Notice the difference between the two types of list.

- **Write each list as a sentence:**

   a) **without a colon**   b) **with a colon.**

1. Citrus fruits
   orange
   lemon
   lime
   grapefruit

a) _____
_____
b) _____
_____

2. Jobs to do
   trim the hedge
   mow the lawn
   prune the roses

a) _____
_____
b) _____
_____

3. Favourite theatres
   the Old Vic
   the Mermaid
   the Garrick

a) _____
_____
b) _____
_____

4. Birds spotted today
   blackbird
   bluetit
   sparrow
   wren

a) _____
_____
b) _____
_____

Now try this!

- **Write five other sentences which contain colons.**
Re-write them so that they do not need colons.

Teachers' note The children could investigate the use of colons in non-fiction texts, deciding why each colon is used (for splitting a sentence into sections or to signal a list).

Developing Literacy
Sentence Level Year 6
© A & C Black 1999

Using semi-colons

In some sentences, two main ideas which are linked to each other are separated by a semi-colon.

> Like me, she enjoys playing chess; unlike me, she is good at it.

• **Re-write these sentences, replacing the connective with a semi-colon.**

1. Sam is good at English but Jenny is good at maths.	
2. Tom swam four lengths but Ben swam six.	
3. Monday's child is fair of face and Tuesday's child is full of grace.	
4. A warm front is approaching the west coast, so it will be sunny tomorrow.	
5. Cats, bats and rats are mammals but dace and plaice are fish.	
6. He arrived at the station late, so he missed the train.	

Now try this!

• **Write five other sentences which contain two main ideas separated by a semi-colon.**

Teachers' note The children could investigate the use of semi-colons in different kinds of texts, particularly dictionaries of proverbs and idioms. They should notice that each of the two parts into which the sentence is split by the semi-colon contains a verb (i.e. each part is a clause).

Developing Literacy
Sentence Level Year 6
© A & C Black 1999

Lists

The items in some lists are separated by 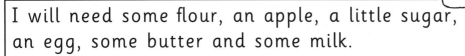 **semi-colons . The items in other lists are separated by commas .**

This is a list of single items.

I will need some flour, an apple, a little sugar, an egg, some butter and some milk.

This is a descriptive list of groups of things.

I will need a large bag of stoneground wholemeal flour; a cup of granulated or caster sugar; one large new-laid egg; a packet of the best unsalted butter and a jug of organic semi-skimmed milk.

• **Punctuate this passage:**

Tim could see what he must do dig up all the dead roots of old rose bushes take away the rubbish and large stones turn over the soil with a spade and use a fork to break up the lumps of clay. He wanted to make a start immediately but he stopped and listed all the tools he needed to collect the equipment he would have to borrow and the materials which he would buy. The tools he would need were a spade a fork a rake a trowel and a small fork. He would borrow the following from his grandfather a dibber for making holes for bulbs secateurs for pruning the bushes worth saving and a riddle for sieving the topmost layer of soil. He listed the things he would buy lime to neutralise the clay soil snowdrop daffodil and hyacinth bulbs and a small bush such as berberis. There were three other things which he would need if he were going to work with lime rubber gloves to protect his hands goggles to keep it out of his eyes and a mask so that he would not breathe in the dust. After the winter he would be able to plant the seeds he had been given larkspur forget-me-nots and lupins.

Now try this!

• **With a partner, read the passage aloud using your voice to show when you are near the end of a list and beginning to read another list.**

Teachers' note The children should complete page 44 before attempting this activity. As a shared reading activity, read out a passage which contains lists and ask the children to indicate when you have begun to read the last item in a list and when you are about to begin reading another.

Developing Literacy
Sentence Level Year 6
© A & C Black 1999

Commas for separating

- **Read each sentence aloud, and decide whether or not the comma is in the right place.** ☐✓ or ☐✗

Work with a partner.

- **If it is in the wrong place, correct it.**

It is a good idea to recycle all the paper we use in school but, we need to make arrangements for storing it.   ☐

Simon does not know, the answer or if he does he is keeping very quiet about it.   ☐

The passenger did not have a ticket, nor did she have any money for the fare.   ☐

Is Martin wearing, new shoes or has he polished his old ones?   ☐

The soloist had a sore, throat so someone else had to take her place.   ☐

Seven people arrived that evening for dinner, but Madhir was expecting only four.   ☐

I suggest, that you make a chicken curry with basmati rice unless any of your guests are vegetarians.   ☐

Now try this!

- **Write six other sentences which have two parts separated by a comma.**

Teachers' note For the extension activity the children could copy sentences from books. During the plenary session they could describe the difference made by the commas.

Developing Literacy
Sentence Level Year 6
© A & C Black 1999

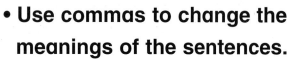

Commas and meaning

- **Use commas to change the meanings of the sentences.**
- **Explain the meanings of the sentences.**

Read the sentences aloud to check their meanings.

The girl said the teacher was naughty.

The girl, said the teacher, was naughty.

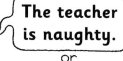

The teacher is naughty.

or

The girl is naughty.

The car I saw was red.

The car I saw was red.

or

He sprang to his feet quickly realising that someone was at the door.

He sprang to his feet quickly realising that someone was at the door.

or

As the sun shone red people moved into the shade.

As the sun shone red people moved into the shade.

or

He bought a goldfish and a cake which he ate on the way home.

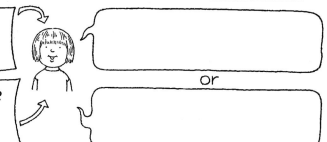

He bought a goldfish and a cake which he ate on the way home.

or

Now try this!

- **Copy six other sentences with commas which affect their meanings.**
- **Copy the sentences without their commas, and explain how their meanings change.**

48

Teachers' note Point out that sometimes one of the sentences in a pair will need no punctuation to give one of its possible meanings.

Developing Literacy
Sentence Level Year 6
© A & C Black 1999

Dashes for separating

A dash can be used to separate a word, phrase or clause from the rest of the sentence.

| There was only one thing to do – laugh. |

Sometimes a comma can be used instead of a dash, but a dash makes the separation stronger.

- **Match the beginnings and endings of sentences.**
- **Copy the complete sentences, with dashes in the correct places.**

Beginnings	Endings
The detective overlooked one important clue	'Greensleeves' and 'Ave Maria'.
	the password is 'eagle'.
I had a choice	to be world champion.
Do not forget this	it was an ordinary small, red saloon which had not been washed for some time.
We ordered our favourite pizza	
She practised for at least twelve hours a day to achieve her dream	the new plaster around the doorway.
There was nothing unusual about the car	cheese and tomato with tuna, sweetcorn and mushrooms.
There were two songs which were special to her	to swim across the fast-flowing river or to be caught.

_____

_____

_____

_____

_____

_____

Now try this!

- **Re-write the sentences using different punctuation marks instead of the dashes.**

Teachers' note The children could also look in various texts for other uses of dashes: for instance, to denote hesitation, an unfinished spoken sentence, or one which the speaker changes part-way through ("I don't know what has happened – I mean I don't know where he is.")

Developing Literacy
Sentence Level Year 6
© A & C Black 1999

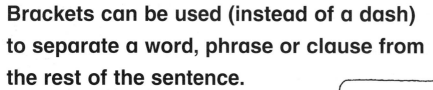

Brackets

Brackets can be used (instead of a dash) to separate a word, phrase or clause from the rest of the sentence.

- **Read the sentences.**
- **Make up the extra information.**
- **Re-read the sentences.**

Brackets can surround an extra piece of information in a sentence.

The old woman (_____) left all her money to charity when she died.

Who was the old woman?

He had four greyhounds (_____ _____) and a whippet.

What was special about two of the greyhounds?

Cut the cake into three layers and spread jam on the bottom one and butter icing (_____ _____) on the middle layer.

Where can I find out how to make butter icing?

We faced another day of rain (_____ _____).

For how many days had it been raining?

Sheena was very proud of her new car (_____).

What kind of car did Sheena have?

The sweet pea growing competition was judged by Mr Harrison (_____ _____).

What made Mr. Harrison a good judge of sweetpeas?

Fry the onions, add the ginger root (_____ _____) and cook for another five minutes.

What should I do to the ginger root before adding it?

Now try this!

- **Write six other sentences containing brackets, cross out the parts in brackets and read the sentences.**
- **Does each sentence still make sense?** ✓ or ✗

Teachers' note The children can learn the term 'parenthesis' to denote the words enclosed by brackets. They should notice that punctuation such as a full stop is placed outside the brackets (except where the parenthesis consists of an entire sentence).

Developing Literacy
Sentence Level Year 6
© A & C Black 1999

Clauses

- **Write six sentences which contain a clause from each set. Join the clauses with a connective word or phrase.**

You can use each clause more than once.

the sun rose in a golden glow behind the rooftops	he was going to be good enough to play for the team
Marco wondered	she could persuade the others that it would be more fun than a disco
Tom was playing in the garden with a flashlight	everyone must have been watching the match, either at the ground or on television
Mrs Johnson asked	the light, shining between the half-opened curtains, woke Ben
there was hardly any traffic in the town centre	Debbie had finished her homework
Meera was hoping to go to the horse-jumping show	the council had introduced a tax on cars to cut down congestion and pollution

_____

_____

_____

_____

_____

_____

_____

_____

_____

_____

Now try this!

- **From books or other texts, copy six sentences which have more than one clause.**
- **Re-write each sentence, changing one of the clauses. You may also need to change the connectives.**

Teachers' note The children should first complete pages 12 and 13. It will help if they first list the connectives they might use, including 'who', 'which' and 'whom'. They can start each sentence with a clause from either set. During the extension activity they could try different ways of changing the meaning of the same sentence.

Developing Literacy
Sentence Level Year 6
© A & C Black 1999

Constructing complex sentences

- **Write complex sentences which contain all the information in the notepads.**
- **Underline the main clauses.**

Wesak commemorates the main events in the life of the Buddha. It is celebrated in May. The date varies. During Wesak Buddhists reflect on the past year. They make resolutions for the following year. Some meditate. They try to think only good thoughts.

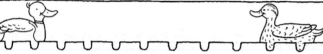

Ducks have webbed feet and wide, flat bills. Most ducks feed on water plants. There are three main types of duck. Diving ducks, like the tufted duck, are the first type. Dabblers, like the mallard, are the second type. The third type is rarer. Fish eating ducks such as sawbills are the third type.

The station was on the far side of the road. There was a lot of traffic. Jessica's train was due to leave in five minutes. She wondered if she would catch it. She spotted a pelican crossing. She pressed the button. The traffic stopped. She could cross the road. She still had to find out which platform to go to.

- **With a partner, edit the complex sentences which you have written.**
- **Re-write them in their improved forms.**

Teachers' note The children should first complete pages 12 and 13. Model the beginning of the first example. Can the children use 'which' to link the first two sentences? Can they think of a phrase to replace 'The date varies' and incorporate it into the sentence? Tell the children to beware of trying to cram too much into one sentence.

Developing Literacy
Sentence Level Year 6
© A & C Black 1999

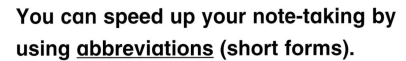

Short forms

You can speed up your note-taking by using <u>abbreviations</u> (short forms).

Use a dictionary.

• **Write the meanings of these standard abbreviations.**

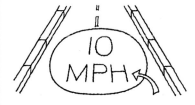

2 Park Rd

_____ _____ _____

CD

sq

_____ _____ _____

5 High St

_____ _____

_____ _____

• **Write your own, non-standard abbreviations for these words.**

children	_____	queen	_____	language	_____
difference	_____	speed	_____	nursery	_____
English	_____	teacher	_____	people	_____
history	_____	computer	_____	science	_____
king	_____	distance	_____	supermarket	_____
month	_____	geography	_____	year	_____
orchestra	_____	illustration	_____	football	_____

Now try this!

• **Write non-standard abbreviations for words you often use in a subject of your choice.**

Teachers' note In the introductory session, the children could read shared texts in which abbreviations are commonly used, for example in mathematics (signs, measures, abbreviations for 'squared', 'cubed', and so on).

Developing Literacy
Sentence Level Year 6
© A & C Black 1999

Shortening sentences

- **Write the brief sentences.**

1
I would like to buy a lovely black dress made of wool in size ten, if you have it.

2
In a grassy hollow at the end of Hartley Avenue, a man on a bicycle has collided with a wall which seems to have rendered him unconscious.

3
I would be most grateful if you could ask an extremely good plumber to come to my house and try to repair a leaking pipe.

4
Out of the twenty helpful people whom we interviewed, ten said that they would be delighted if the city centre were to be pedestrianised.

5
Hughes kicked the ball, which soared into the air and sailed over the roof of the stadium into the road outside, where a passer-by picked it up in amazement.

6
The comedian told such hilariously funny jokes that the people in the theatre held their sides and shook with laughter.

1

2

3

4

5

6

 Now try this!

- **Copy five very long sentences from books.**
- **Re-write the sentences as brief sentences.**

Teachers' note Discuss the purpose of summarising the spoken words on the page (to give information briefly) and of summarising fiction (to give an outline of the main events of a story).

**Developing Literacy
Sentence Level Year 6
© A & C Black 1999**

Avoiding repetition

- **Re-write the news so that the newsreader does not repeat things or use several words where one would do.**

1

At 9am this morning the boys and girls were ready to show us the pictures they had painted.

Repetition Police

9am **is** morning.
Boys + girls = children
Pictures they have painted = their paintings.

1

At 9am the children were ready to show us their paintings.

2

Cars, vans, trucks and buses filled the street as a quite considerable number of people on foot tried to walk across it.

2

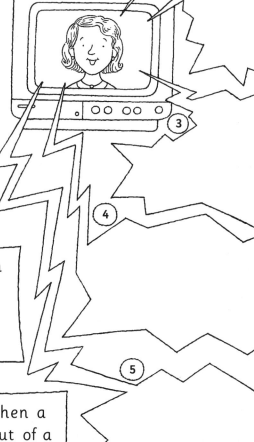

3

In the north-west of England a man in Manchester is the lucky winner who has won tonight's star prize.

3

4

Our regular viewers who watch this programme every day will recognise the familiar face of Sam Jones.

4

5

The accident happened when a car reversed backwards out of a driveway. Sam Jones is on the spot, where it happened, with two witnesses who saw it.

5

Now try this!

- **Look for repetition in a piece of your own writing.**
- **Re-write it without any repetition.**

Teachers' note This activity could be linked with text-level work on writing recounts and reports.

Developing Literacy
Sentence Level Year 6
© A & C Black 1999

Summaries

• **Use the chart to record the main points of the news report.**

Complete the chart in note form.

A planning application to build accommodation for 240 students in Redfield Road has met with opposition from local residents. The application, made by Toptown University, is to build a four-storey block, housing 240 students with a car park at the rear. But residents fear that this will bring extra noise and disturbance in the early hours of the morning and cause parking problems. Councillor Jack Jones said, 'The residents are right to oppose this application. It would bring misery to their lives. I fully support them.'

One resident thinks that a four-storey building will block light from their homes. She said, 'Why build more student accommodation when a recent survey showed that applications for places at universities are down by 20%?'

Another resident was equally adamant: 'These narrow roads cannot cope with the extra traffic which the flats will bring to the area.'

A spokesman for the university said, 'Every autumn we are faced with many students without accommodation. There are others who rent flats and houses which are in very poor condition. We want students to begin their studies without the worry of looking for somewhere to stay. We want them to live in decent conditions. We always try to keep local residents informed and to respond to their concerns. We have had an open meeting with the developers and local people during which many of their concerns were noted.'

What is the argument about?

Who are for the plan and why?

Who are against the plan and why?

The issue	For (and reasons)	Against (and reasons)	How the problem is being tackled

Now try this!

• **Write a summary of the issue using the main points on your chart.**

Write the summary in complete sentences.

Teachers' note The children could use charts like the one provided to structure their note-taking and to inform their summaries of other reports in newspapers.

Developing Literacy
Sentence Level Year 6
© A & C Black 1999

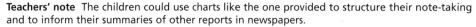

Auxiliary verbs

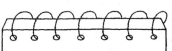

You can change the tense of a sentence by changing the auxiliary verbs.

- Highlight the auxiliary verbs in each sentence.
- Re-write the sentence in a different tense, by changing the auxiliary verbs.

Auxiliary verbs
have, has, had
am, are, is was, were
can could shall, will should, would

> I can now afford the new tracksuit which I saw in the shop.

I could then afford the new tracksuit which I had seen in the shop.

> She will not let her brother read the comic; that is why he is crying.

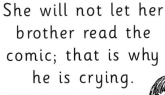

_____

> There were two men riding horses, but I could not see their faces.

_____

> It had been sunny, but now it was starting to rain.

_____

- Re-write both sets of sentences, changing the first auxiliary verb to 'might' (or 'might have', or 'might be').
- What do you notice?

Teachers' note The children could also explore the ways in which verbs change to agree with auxiliary verbs: for example 'I shall buy', but 'I have bought'.

Developing Literacy
Sentence Level Year 6
© A & C Black 1999

Conditional clauses

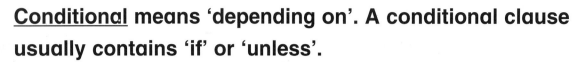

Conditional means 'depending on'. A conditional clause usually contains 'if' or 'unless'.

Example: I will help you <u>if I can</u>.

- **Complete the conditional clause in each sentence.**

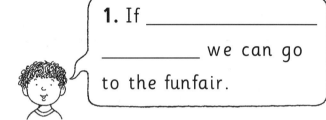

1. If _____ _____ we can go to the funfair.

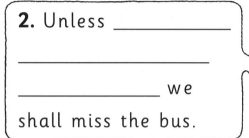

2. Unless _____ _____ _____ we shall miss the bus.

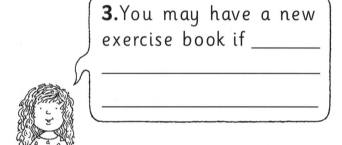

3. You may have a new exercise book if _____ _____ _____

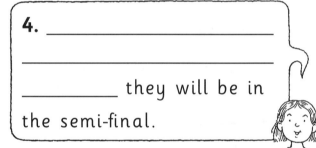

4. _____ _____ _____ they will be in the semi-final.

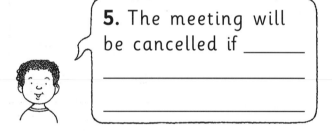

5. The meeting will be cancelled if _____ _____ _____

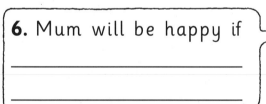

6. Mum will be happy if _____ _____

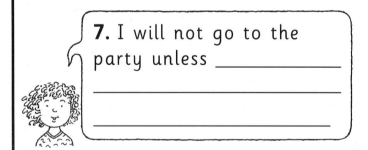

7. I will not go to the party unless _____ _____ _____

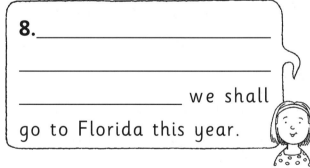

8. _____ _____ _____ we shall go to Florida this year.

Now try this!

- **Re-write sentences 1, 5, 6 and 7 in the past tense.**
- **Use auxiliary verbs like <u>could</u> and <u>would</u>.**

Teachers' note The children should first revise auxiliary verbs (page 57). They could look for conditionals in a shared text and make notes of the words which they find in connection with them, such as 'would', 'could', 'can', 'if' and 'unless'.

Developing Literacy
Sentence Level Year 6
© A & C Black 1999

Conditional songs and rhymes

• **Write the auxiliary verbs in the gaps.**

If wishes were horses
Beggars _____ ride;
If turnips _____ watches
I _____ wear one by
my side.

If I had a hammer,
I _____ hammer in the morning,
I _____ hammer in the
evening...

I would, if I _____
if I couldn't how
_____ I?

If all the world were paper,
and all the sea were ink,
if all the trees _____ bread
and cheese,
what _____ we have to drink?

If the oak is out before
the ash,
then we _____ only
have a splash;
if the ash _____ out
before the oak,
then we _____ surely
have a soak.

If all the sea _____ one sea,
what a great sea that _____ be!
If all the trees _____ one tree,
what a great tree that _____ be!

If the mocking bird
_____ sing
Papa's _____ to
buy you a diamond ring.

If I _____ a donkey that would not
go, _____ I beat him? Oh, no, no!
I _____ put him in the barn and give
him some corn,
the best little donkey that ever _____
born.

Now try this!

• **Re-write each song or rhyme in a different tense.**
• **Underline the conditional clauses.**

Teachers' note The children should first complete pages 57 and 58. They could make a display of the words of songs which contain conditionals, noticing that 'would' and 'should' are often abbreviated ('d).

Developing Literacy
Sentence Level Year 6
© A & C Black 1999

Conditional verbs

• **Match the clauses.**

If the dog is female	it will have been posted yesterday.
If the dog had been female	it would have been posted on Saturday.
If the letter comes today	we shall call it Jessie.
If the letter came on Monday	there might have been a hosepipe ban.
If the summer is dry	you should have bought it here.
If the summer had been dry	I can see over the fence.
If you want a ticket	we would have called it Jessie.
If you had wanted a ticket	there might be a hosepipe ban.
If I stand on tiptoe	you should buy it here.
If I stood on tiptoe	no one will recognise me.
If I had stood on tiptoe	no one would have recognised me.
If I wear a hat	I could have seen over the fence.
If I wore a hat	no one would recognise me.
If I had worn a hat	I could see over the fence.

Now try this!

• **Re-write each of these sentences in two different tenses.**

If you hide here no one will find you.

_____

_____

If I pick enough blackberries, I shall bake a pie.

_____

_____

If the dress fits, she will wear it.

_____

_____

Teachers' note The children should first complete pages 57-59. During the plenary session, the children could contribute to a chart to show the different tenses of conditional verbs.

Developing Literacy
Sentence Level Year 6
© A & C Black 1999

Just suppose

• Complete these conditional ideas in any way you like.

Example:
Suppose there were inhabitants on Mars: how would they breathe?

Imagine you could fly:

Let's say there is a monster in the lake:

I wish I were an astronaut:

What if electricity had never been invented?

Consider a world without colours:

He predicted that someone would invent

Picture a world where there was no crime:

She dreamed of the day when she would

• Choose one of the ideas on this page.

• Write two paragraphs about it, using conditional verbs.

Teachers' note The children should first complete pages 57–60.

Developing Literacy
Sentence Level Year 6
© A & C Black 1999

Formal writing

- **Read the members' suggestions for the tennis club rules.**
- **Re-write the rules in the <u>impersonal</u> voice.**

The members wrote the rules in the <u>imperative</u> form.

Wear tennis shoes on the courts.

Put the net away if you are the last people to use a court.

Please make sure that the club-house is locked if you are the last to leave.

Please pay your subscription by 30th April.

Please take your turn to make the tea.

Please leave quietly so as not to disturb local residents.

<u>Members should wear tennis shoes on the courts.</u>

_____

_____

_____

_____

_____

_____

_____

_____

_____

_____

_____

_____

_____

_____

_____

_____

_____

_____

Do not wear coloured T shirts.

Do not take glasses or bottles on to the courts.

If others are waiting please limit your game to three sets.

You may sign in one non-member per day.

Do not bring animals on to the club premises.

Put all valuables in a locker.

Now try this!

- **Using ideas written by your group in the imperative form, write a set of formal rules in the impersonal voice for using your school playground.**

Teachers' note The children should first complete pages 22–25. Before this activity it will be useful to compile a list of sentence openings, to avoid beginning every sentence with 'Members...'. Examples include: 'It would be appreciated..', 'We request...' and '.... should/should not.'

**Developing Literacy
Sentence Level Year 6
© A & C Black 1999**

Using passive verbs

• **Write a description of this restaurant using passive verbs.**

The passive is used when the actions are important, rather than the people doing them.

① People know this restaurant for its fresh fish.

② The chef uses them in dishes such as plaice mornay.

③ He grills cod or deep fries it in batter.

④ Someone delivers fresh meat daily.

⑤ Someone local makes the Cumberland sausages which they serve.

⑥ Someone buys fresh vegetables from local markets and cooks them to perfection.

⑦ They display desserts in a cold cabinet.

⑧ Someone serves puddings which someone has made at home.

⑨ They serve cheese which someone local had made.

⑩ They serve coffee in the beautiful oak-beamed lounge.

<u>This restaurant is known for its fresh fish.</u>

_____

_____

_____

_____

_____

_____

_____

_____

_____

_____

_____

_____

_____

_____

_____

_____

_____

Now try this!

• **Make notes about your school canteen or a restaurant you know. Write about it in the passive, for a good food guide.**

Teachers' note The children should first complete pages 18–21. Provide examples of texts which are written mainly in the passive voice and discuss the effect of this and the reason for it.

Developing Literacy
Sentence Level Year 6
© A & C Black 1999

Better sentences

- **Re-write these clumsy sentences.**
- **The first one has been done for you.**

> You might need to add, delete or change some words.

She bought the dress and she found that it did not fit when she tried it on, so she went back to the shop to see if they would exchange it.

Having bought the dress, tried it on and found that it did not fit, she went back to the shop to ask for an exchange.

Ella liked chips and so she ordered fish and chips, and so did Sam, but Carl did not like them so he ordered fish and peas.

_____

_____

_____

St. Martin's church is a hundred years old, but there is an even older church in Highville; that is St. Hugh's which is two hundred years old.

_____

_____

_____

I had never been to Ireland and this was my first visit to Dublin, where my grandmother was born (she lived there until she was ten and then her family moved to Liverpool).

_____

_____

_____

Now try this!

- **Make a list of words which are useful in long sentences: for example, having, which, who, whom, where, when.**
- **Re-write a piece of your own work using long sentences. Do they improve it?**

Teachers' note Before the activity the children could read texts which contain long sentences and notice the words and punctuation which are used. It might be necessary to revise colons, semi-colons, dashes and brackets.

Developing Literacy
Sentence Level Year 6
© A & C Black 1999